John E. Llewellyn-Jones

BODY PLANS
Animals from the inside

fish · frog · lizard · pigeon
rabbit · earthworm · spider
starfish · butterfly · snail

CAMBRIDGE UNIVERSITY PRESS

Cambridge

London New York New Rochelle Melbourne Sydney

To my mother

Author's acknowledgements

I would like to thank my wife Marianne and my children Céline and David for their patience and understanding during the past year. Their encouragement has been a great help during the hours spent in planning, drawing, redrawing, colouring, cutting and sticking the model animals to be found in this book.

I would also like to thank the following people for all the help and advice they have given me in the preparation of this book: T. Wallace, B. Wallace, K. Chapman, P. Palmer, C. Kulik, D. Evans, W. Langworthy, D. Bayne, J. Robins, J. Shalders and especially Tristan Rees-Roberts. I would also like to thank C. Burwell and staff for the regular use of their photocopier and lastly the staff and pupils of Chalvedon School who have in one way or another helped me in the preparation of the material for this book.

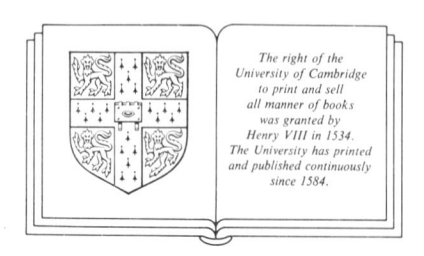

The right of the University of Cambridge to print and sell all manner of books was granted by Henry VIII in 1534. The University has printed and published continuously since 1584.

Published by the Press Syndicate of the University of Cambridge
The Pitt Building, Trumpington Street, Cambridge CB2 1RP
32 East 57th Street, New York, NY 10022, USA
10 Stamford Road, Oakleigh, Melbourne 3166, Australia

© Cambridge University Press 1986

First published 1986
Reprinted 1986

Printed in Great Britain by David Green Printers Ltd.,
Kettering, Northamptonshire

British Library Cataloguing in Publication Data
Llewellyn-Jones, John
  Body plans: animals from the inside.
  1. Anatomy—Juvenile literature
  I. Title
  591.4   QL806.5

ISBN 0 521 31711 8

Fish

Many types of animal have adapted to life in water but fish are the most successful of all. Some inhabit the sea, others fresh water and there are even some species which can live in both. Fish can also exist in all kinds of unfavourable or foul-water conditions. Some species are able to breathe air and can survive for periods of time on land. Mudskippers leave the sea at low tide carrying a supply of water in the gills which allows them to breathe while on land. However, they have to return to the sea from time to time to renew their water supply. The climbing perch of southern Asia can travel over land pulling itself along by the edges of its gill covers. The gills inside are especially adapted for allowing it to breathe atmospheric air.

Fish are divided into a number of groups, the two main divisions being the cartilagenous and the bony fish. The sharks and their relatives the rays belong to the first of these two groups and altogether there are about three thousand different species. As the name implies, bony fish have a skeleton made of bone and these fish are much more numerous than their counterparts with cartilagenous skeletons. Biologists have estimated that there may be as many as twenty-three thousand different species of bony fish.

Because of the wide range of aquatic habitats which fish live in, they show a great variety of body shapes. Some are long and thin, others short and fat. Puffer fish are able to take on a spherical shape by blowing up their bodies with air. However, most fish conform to a typical torpedo shape where the body is streamlined for easy and quick movement through the water. These fish have a cylindrically-shaped body with a pointed head end, a wider mid-part and a rear end tapering towards the tail fin. The main power for swimming comes from the body muscles. As these contract, the body is bent from side to side and this, together with the movement of the tail fin, causes the fish to move forward. There are also specialised fins sticking out from the body at specific regions and these help in maintaining stability as the fish moves through the water. They also help in turning, making movements upwards and downwards and in braking or slowing down.

Fish are able to extract oxygen from the water by means of gills. These are found on both sides of the head, and are protected, in bony fish, by a flap of skin called an operculum. The gills of sharks and their close relatives are not protected in the same way and can be seen as a series of slits on each side of the head. Gills are organs especially adapted for breathing in water because of their large surface area and a rich blood supply. Water is drawn across the gills and as it passes over their surface, oxygen enters the fish's blood stream. In the same way, carbon dioxide leaves the gills and passes into the surrounding water.

Many fish are brightly coloured and this is particularly true of those species living in tropical seas. In some species, colours become important at specific times of the year, as in the stickleback during the breeding season. Some fish are able to change colour in order to achieve a better camouflage. Other fish use both camouflage colours and an unusual shape in order to hide themselves amongst the habitat in which they live. For example, a fish called the Sea Dragon lives in the waters around Australia. It is a small fish with ragged flaps of skin hanging from different parts of its body which make it look like a piece of floating sea weed thus protecting it from predators.

In the majority of fish, the female lays eggs in the water which are fertilised by a male. Sometimes fertilisation takes place inside the female but this is unusual. Many fish show a complicated courtship behaviour and in some cases this results in nest building activities. Other fish show unusual ways of looking after the eggs once they have been fertilised. For example, female tilapia fish take the eggs into their mouths where they hatch. The young fish stay in the mouth and are protected there until they can look after themselves. Fish produce large numbers of eggs. It has been estimated that a single female cod will produce seven million eggs and a ling as many as twenty-eight million in a single breeding season. Most of these are eaten and only a few develop into adult fish.

Fish

colour and assembly

Colour the stickleback's **external body shape** in the following way. Colour back and sides green. In the Spring, the male becomes very brightly coloured. It has a red belly and chin and bright blue eyes. The fins are pale blue or green. Use this information to colour the rest of the body shape.

Key and colours to numbered parts

1. gullet (oesophagus) (green)
2. stomach (green)
3. intestine (green)
4. cloaca (green)
5. kidney (brown)
6. testes (yellow)
7. liver lobes (brown)
8. heart (red)
9. swim (air) bladder (blue)
10. backbone (spine) and ribs—these have already been coloured black
11. gill (red)
12. gill cover (operculum) (green)
13. dorsal fin
14. tail (caudal) fin
15. anal (ventral) fin } (pale blue or green)
16. pelvic spine
17. pectoral fin

Assembly instructions

Colour the parts 1–17 using the colours suggested above. Cut out the parts and then fix into your book or onto a piece of card or paper in the following order:—

Stick down the **internal body section** towards the left hand side of your paper.

Now stick the various body organs onto the lettered, shaded areas marked on the **internal body section** in the following order:

the heart by tab **A**
the gullet by tab **B**
the testis by tab **C**
the liver by tab **D**
the gill by tab **E**

Cut around the operculum on the **external body shape** from 12 to 12 and open slightly.

Fix the **pectoral fin** onto the **external body shape** by its tab **G**.

Fix the **external body shape** by tab **F** onto the lettered, shaded area marked **F** on the **internal body section**.

NOTE. If you have fixed the external body shape correctly the gills should lie just underneath the operculum.

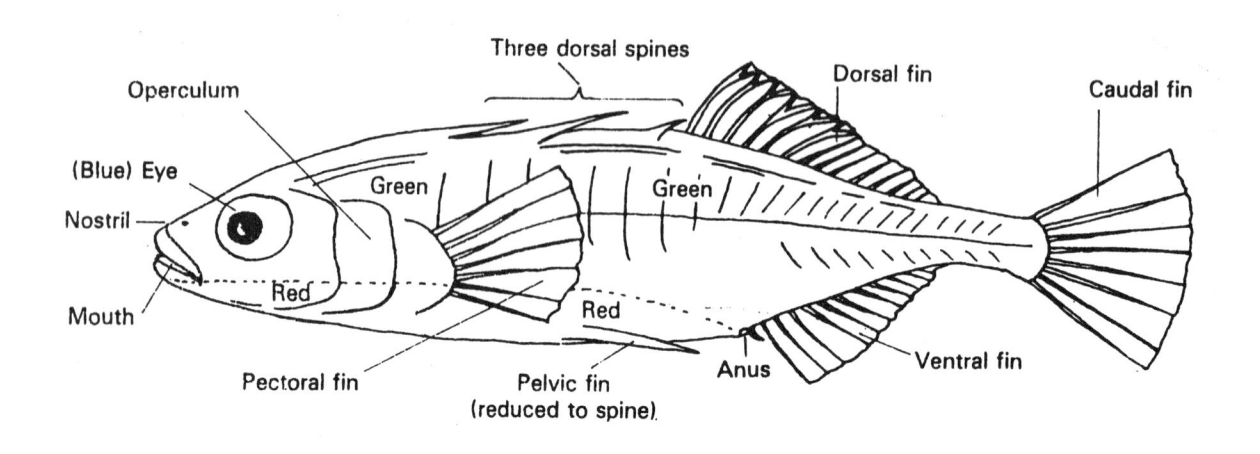

Write the title and date above the completed cut out.

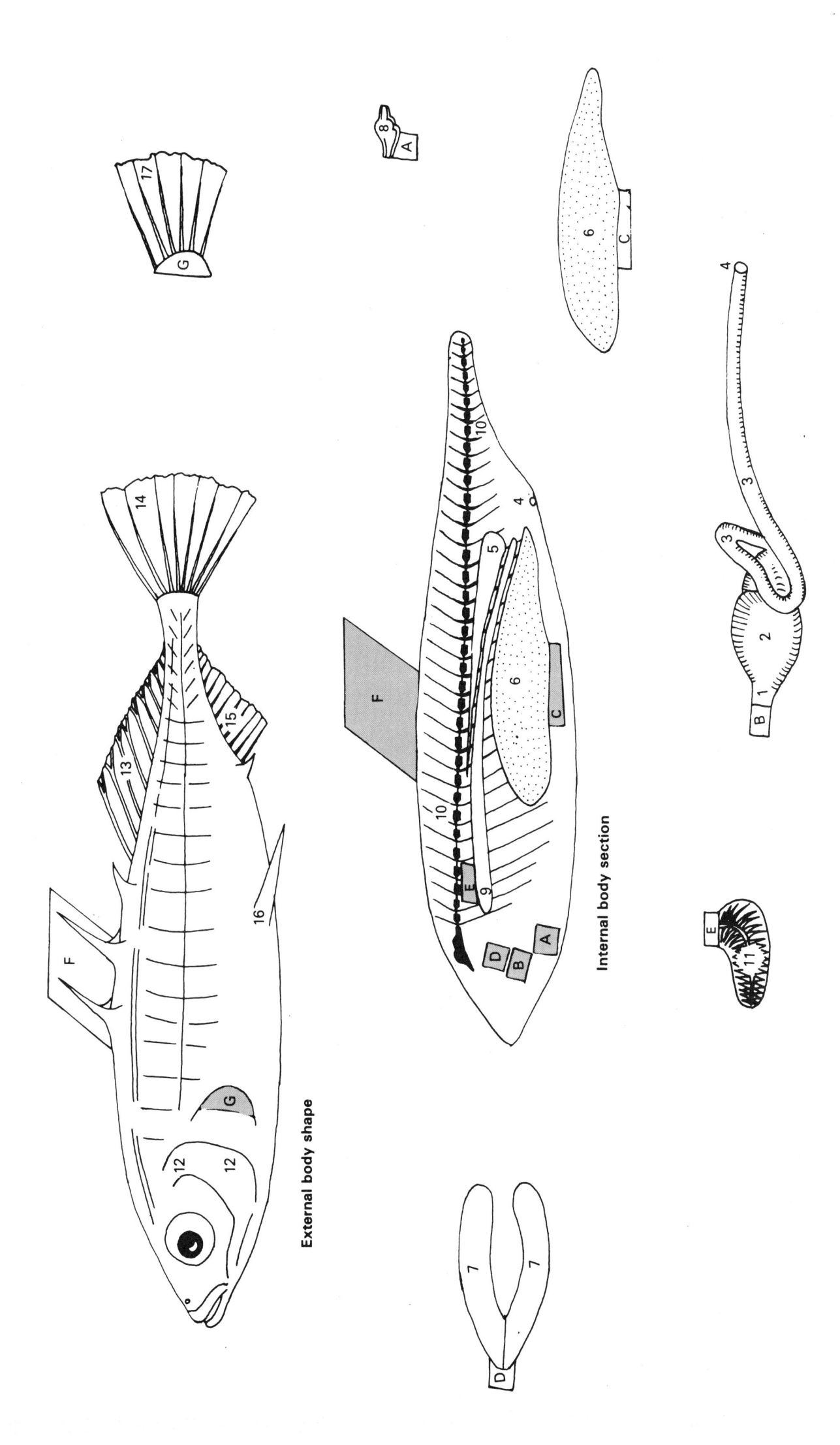

External body shape

Internal body section

Frog

background information

Frogs belong to a group of animals called Amphibia of which there are about two thousand different species living in the world today. They tend to live in confined habitats and most of them cannot exist far from water. Some desert toads survive in tropical regions by burrowing in the ground and by special adaptations which allow them to live in dry conditions. There are three main groups of amphibia: the newts and salamanders, the frogs and toads and a small group of tropical, limbless types which burrow in the soil rather like worms.

Frogs are common in most parts of the world except the southern part of South America, New Zealand and on oceanic islands. All frogs have the same basic shape, although they vary in size from the giant Goliath frog of tropical Africa to the tiny arrowpoison frog from Cuba. They tend to inhabit moist, damp conditions such as marshes, swamps and ditches, where they spend most of their time in the undergrowth. They have powerful hind limbs adapted for both swimming and leaping. The webs on the hind feet provide a large surface area for pushing against the water. Frogs crawl on rough ground. The eyes, which are on top of the head, protrude above the water while swimming. Each has a protective, moveable lid and this can be withdrawn into the skull for further protection. The eardrums can be seen on the side of the head behind and below the eyes.

All frogs are carnivorous, feeding on insects including beetles and flies. They also feed on worms when they can find them. They have an especially adapted tongue which can be shot out in a half circle and the prey is trapped in the sticky saliva covering its surface. As the tongue is pulled back, the prey is crushed against the roof of the mouth. The skull of the frog also has a row of tiny, closely set teeth on its upper jaw with which it crushes its food.

Frogs have a loose-fitting, thin, moist skin which is supplied with a network of blood vessels. The skin is used for breathing and oxygen is absorbed through its surface into the blood from the water. The nostrils are situated in such a way that air can be breathed into the lungs even while the frog is swimming under the surface of the water. Valves inside the nostrils stop water entering.

The frog's colours often act as camouflage in its natural surroundings. These colours can be made darker or lighter by expanding and contracting the pigment spots in the skin. Many tree frogs living amongst tropical vegetation take on a bright green colour which becomes much duller when the animals move into shaded areas. Some tropical species are very brightly coloured and their skins produce poisons which are fatal to humans and other animals. In this case, these bright colours act as warnings designed to advertise the dangerous nature of the animals. South American Indians have taken advantage of this and certain tribes still extract these poisons for their hunting arrows.

All frogs depend upon water for breeding and this is even true of the specialised desert toads which reproduce quickly at the beginning of the rainy season. During mating, the male joins the larger female, climbing onto her back and clasping her firmly around the middle. The two sexes remain together for several days while the female lays eggs at regular intervals. Immediately after the eggs are fertilised externally by the male shedding sperm over them in the water, a thin layer of protective jelly swells around them. During the next few days, the yolk in each egg develops into a tadpole, with external gills. The tadpoles wriggle free of the jelly after a few days and they usually attach themselves to pieces of pond weed by a small sucker. After a period of time, the external gills change into internal ones, protected by a structure called an operculum. Now the tadpoles start feeding on vegetation using a pair of horny, toothed-jaws. Over the next few weeks hind limbs form followed by front limbs. Lungs form and the tadpole changes from being herbivorous to carnivorous. It now starts to feed on insect larvae and crustaceans. The tail is reabsorbed and the small frog climbs out of the water onto the land. This now feeds amongst the grass and undergrowth close to the water's edge and develops into an adult frog.

Frog

Colour the frog's underside, chin, arms, sides of the **internal body section** and legs pale yellow and then go over the chin, arms, and legs very lightly with green.

Key and colours to numbered parts

1. oesophagus (gullet) (green)
2. stomach (green)
3. small intestine (green)
4. rectum (green)
5. cloaca (green)
6. pancreas (yellow)
7. spleen (red)
8. bladder (yellow)
9. kidneys (brown)
10. testes (yellow)
11. liver lobes (brown)
12. gall bladder (green)
13. lungs (orange)
14. heart (red)
15. orbits (eye socket) (pale green)
16. tongue (red)
17. lower jaw (yellow)
18. upper jaw (yellow)
19. nuptial pad of male thumb (yellow/green)
20. inferior vena cava (blue)
21. veins (blue)
22. arteries (red)
23. dorsal aorta (red)
24. veins (blue)

Assembly instructions

Colour the parts **1–24** using the colours suggested above. Cut out the parts and then fix into your book or onto a piece of card or paper in the following order:—

Stick down the **internal body section** in the centre of your paper.

Now stick the various body organs onto the lettered, shaded areas marked on the **internal body section** in the following order:

the testes by tab **A**
the alimentary canal by tab **B1**
the bladder by tab **C**
the lungs by tab **D**
the liver lobes by tab **B2** over the tab for the alimentary canal **B1**
the heart by tab **E**
the lower jaw by tab **F**

Now stick on the **nuptial pad** over the lettered, shaded area by the tab **G**.

Stick the **underside** in position by its tab so that all the internal organs are covered.

Write the title and date above the completed cut out.

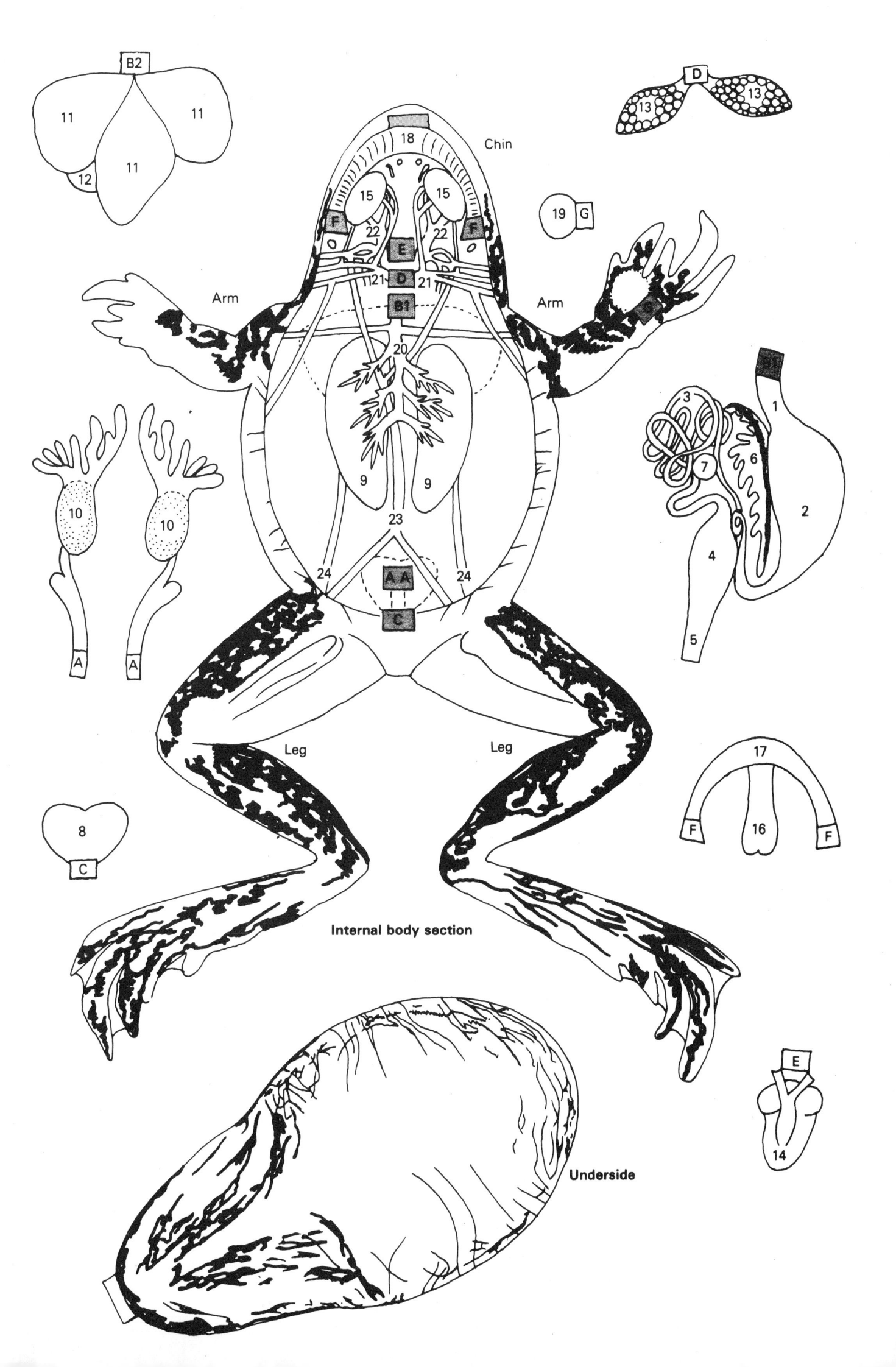

Internal body section

Underside

Lizard

There are about six thousand different species of reptile living in the world today. The majority live in warmer parts, although two species, the common lizard and the adder, are found as far north as the Arctic Circle. There are four sub-groups of reptile: lizards, snakes, turtles and tortoises and crocodiles. These sub-groups are different in shape and structure, although the basic internal body plan is the same. Lizards live in a wide variety of land habitats, ranging from desert environments to tropical rainforests. There is even one species of lizard on the Galapagos Islands which spends much of its time in the sea or basking on rocks. Tortoises are also land animals but their close relatives, the terrapins and turtles, are aquatic as are the crocodiles. Snakes are specially adapted for life on land. They have no limbs and move by means of powerful body muscles. They live in a wide variety of habitats and many of them are expert climbers. Even among the snakes, there are a few species which live in water and some of the sea snakes are very poisonous.

Lizards have a common body shape which is usually cylindrical. There is a pointed head and a long, tapering tail. The body is raised up off the ground on four legs, each ending in a clawed foot. This shape is sometimes modified depending on the habitat. For example, chameleons are flattened from side to side to help them move between the leaves amongst which they live. They also have a coiled prehensile tail, an adaptation for climbing amongst twigs and branches. Many desert-living lizards such as the skinks have shorter, fatter bodies and the tail is often used for storing fat.

The majority of lizards are carnivorous but there are some herbivorous types. Iguana lizards from South America feed on leaves and fruit, and the Galapagos sea lizards browse on sea weed. Chameleons catch insects by shooting out a long, sticky-tipped tongue. These lizards also have stereoscopic vision to help them judge the distance between themselves and the prey they are attempting to catch.

Lizards have a dry, scaly skin which helps in protection and also prevents the loss of excess water from the body. The skin is flaked off from time to time as new scales are produced underneath. Many lizards have bold, bright colour patterns on the skin which helps in camouflaging the animals in their natural surroundings. In addition to this, some lizards, such as chameleons and anolids, are able to change colour in order to match the background in which they find themselves.

Unlike mammals and birds, reptiles are not able to maintain a constant body temperature. The temperature of their blood varies with that of the surroundings and, because of this, those species living in temperate countries have to hibernate during the cold winter months in order to survive. Although they are unable to control their internal body temperature in the way mammals and birds do, many lizards show different behavioural patterns which allow them to warm up and cool down at different times of the day. For example, agama lizards in tropical Africa bask in the warmth of the sun during the early part of the day but, as the air temperature increases, they seek the shade of rocks or other structures where they are able to cool down by radiating their body heat back into the shady surroundings.

The bright colours of many male lizards play an important part in breeding and territory behaviour. Special flaps of skin, including dewlaps and crests, are also important during courtship. After attracting the female, mating takes place followed by internal fertilisation. The eggs are buried under soil or sand and hatch out later on, often as a result of warmth from the sun. Some lizards, such as chameleons, give birth to live young and this is probably an adaptation to an arboreal life. Turtles, which have become aquatic in habit, still have to come ashore to lay their eggs, usually in sand at the top of an oceanic island beach. However, as soon as the eggs hatch, the baby turtles head straight for the sea.

Lizard

colour and assembly

Colour the lizard's **external body shape** and the tail on the **internal body section** in the following way. Colour the back, sides, head and legs light brown, the belly and chin pale yellow and the eye orange.

Key and colours to numbered parts

1. gullet (green)
2. stomach (green)
3. small intestine (green)
4. rectum (green)
5. spleen (red)
6. pancreas (yellow)
7. cloaca (green)
8. bladder (yellow)
9. kidneys (brown)
10. ovaries (yellow)
11. liver lobe (brown)
12. lungs (orange)
13. trachea (wind pipe) (orange)
14. tongue (red)
15. heart (red)
16. brain (black)
17. spine and spinal cord—these have already been coloured black
18. muscles (red)

Assembly instructions

Colour the parts 1–18 using the colours suggested above. Cut out the parts and then fix into your book or onto a piece of card or paper in the following order:—

Stick down the **internal body section** and tail in the centre of the paper.

Now stick the various body organs onto the lettered, shaded areas marked on the **internal body section** in the following order:

the alimentary canal by tab **A**
the lung by tab **B**
the heart by tab **C**
the kidney by tab **D**

Now stick the **external body shape** by tab **E** onto the lettered, shaded area marked **E** on the **internal body section** so that all the internal organs are covered.

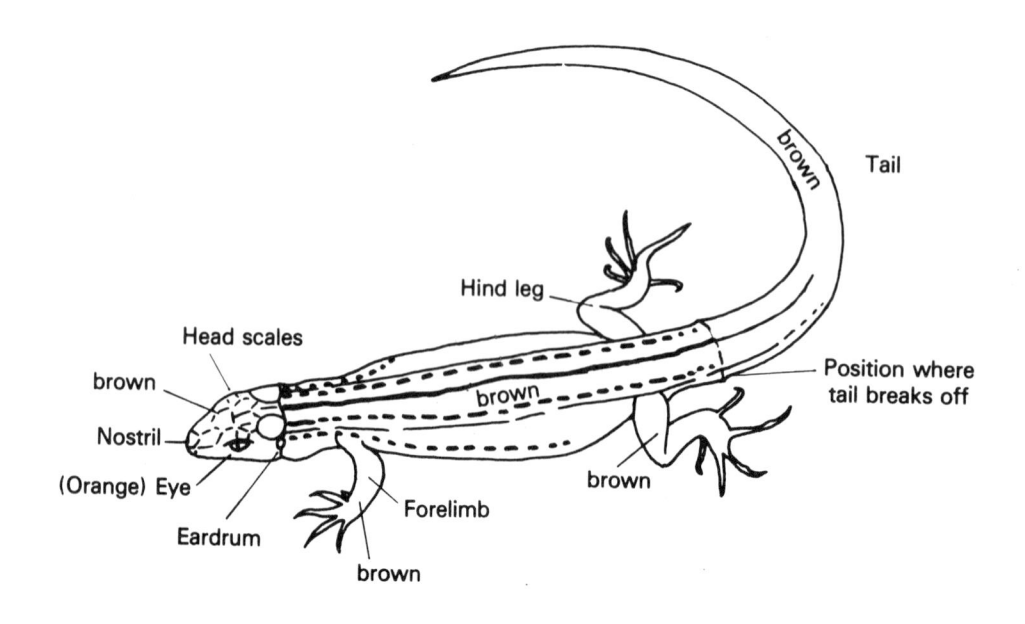

Write the title and date above the completed cut out.

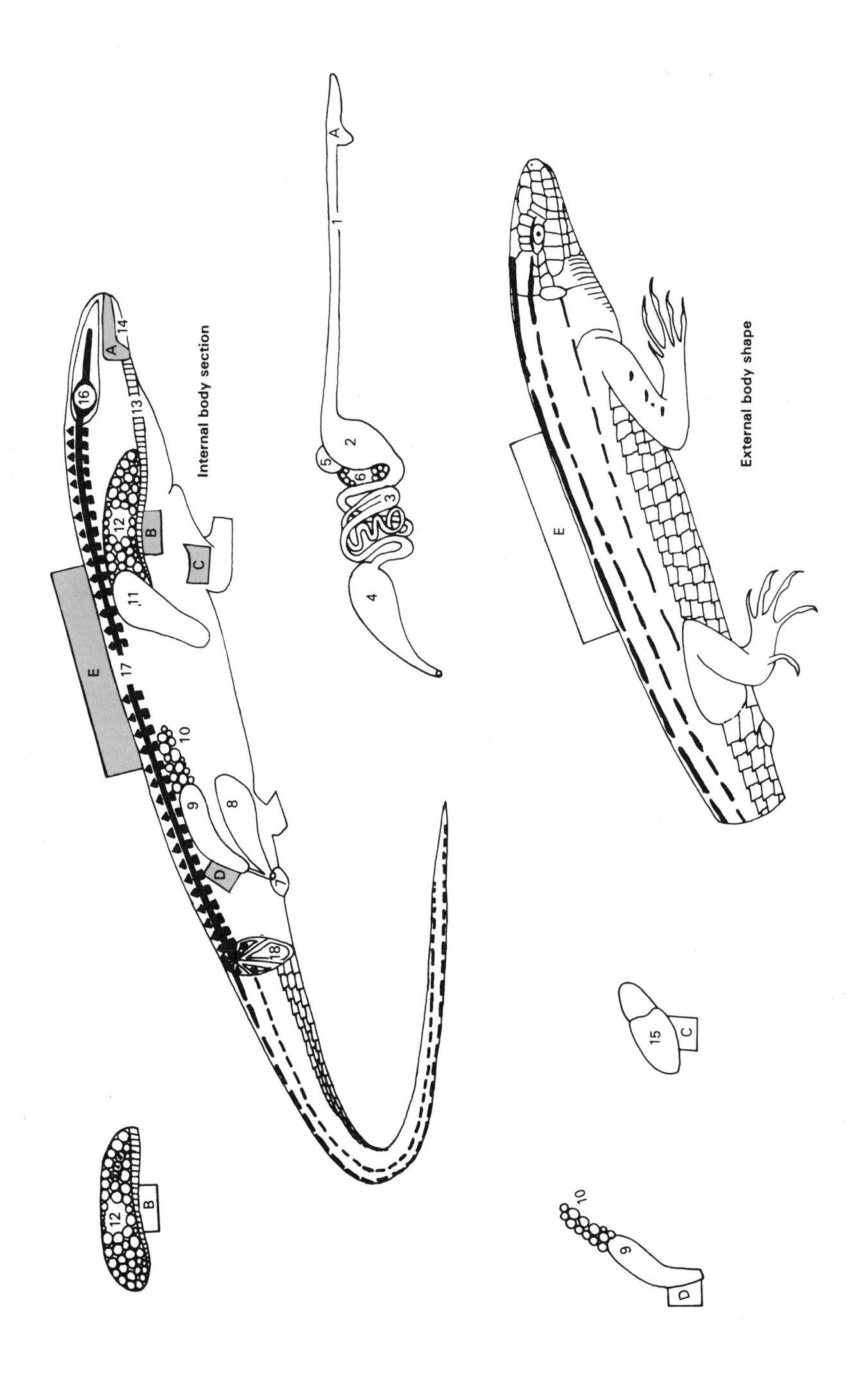

Internal body section

External body shape

Bird

It has been estimated that there are as many as one hundred billion birds living in the world today. They are found in a wide variety of habitats ranging from the coldest polar regions to the hottest deserts. They live both at sea level and at high altitudes and they have colonised some of the remotest islands. Birds have been able to invade this range of environments because although the basic body plan remains the same, it shows a wide variety of special features which can become modified for many different kinds of habitat. For example, birds show differences in size, body shape, and beak, wing and foot structures.

The skin of birds is loose and dry and there are no sweat glands. A feature of the skin is the development of feathers and this is one of the main characteristics of birds. Feathers provide a covering to the body and they help in insulation and flight. They also function in providing protective coloration and, in many species, they help in display and courtship by the male. The feathers are moulted either at certain stages in the life history or seasonally and new ones are produced to replace them.

The front limbs of most birds are specially modified as wings and are covered with feathers. Each main wing feather is made up of a long shaft and a vane which contains numerous parallel barbs. The barbs are inter-connected by hooked barbules. The structure of the feathers and the way they are arranged provides a complete covering to the wings which in turn gives an aerodynamic surface. In some birds the wings have become reduced in size over long periods of time and such birds are now 'flightless'. The ostrich, rhea and emu are examples of this. Instead of relying on flight, these birds use their powerful legs to enable them to run quickly. In the case of penguins, the fore limbs are shaped like flippers, an adaptation to swimming under water.

Birds fly in different ways. Some, such as pigeons, use a flapping type of flight and others either soar on warm air rising upwards or on air currents moving off the surface of the sea. These different types of flight require different shaped wings, vultures have broad wings to help catch thermal currents whereas albatroses have long, thin wings for gliding in the windy conditions above the surface of the sea. Certain birds such as humming birds are able to beat their wings as quickly as fifty times per second and this allows them to hover in a stationary position or, in some cases, to fly backwards. Birds fly at different speeds but the majority are capable of flying at between fifty and eighty kilometres per hour. Some birds, such as swifts, can fly as fast as one hundred and eighty kilometres per hour and certain hawks, such as the peregrin falcon, can probably achieve speeds even greater than this when diving onto their prey from a great height. Very acute vision is necessary for flight. The skeleton is made up of hollow, air-filled bones and, in addition to this, the body contains a number of air sacs as well as a large pair of lungs. All these structures help to lighten the bird's weight and this in turn helps in conserving energy during flight.

Many birds show a complicated pattern of behaviour during courtship. The males are often brightly coloured to attract females and, in addition, these colours help them in maintaining their territory which they defend vigorously. Part of the breeding behaviour involves the building of some kind of nest and these structures differ greatly in their size and shape and also where they are made. Some birds nest on the ground, using only a minimum of nesting materials while others build large and complicated structures high above the ground in the tops of trees. Others breed in large colonies, on rock faces or in burrows in the ground and there are even some species which build complicated mud nests in which to lay their eggs.

Once mating has taken place and the nest is built, the female lays its eggs which are then incubated, sometimes by both parents in turn, until the young ones hatch. The number of eggs laid varies from one species to another and in the case of some of the larger birds of prey, only one or two youngsters are reared. Parental care is well developed in many birds and the young are looked after carefully over quite a long period of time.

Bird

Colour the pigeon's **external body shape** in the following way. Colour the body and wings blue-grey. The rump between the wings should be left white. The two black wing bars are already coloured in. The head and neck should be coloured dark grey with areas of purple and green on the side of the neck. The beak is black with a white patch. The eye ring is red and the legs pink with dark red scales. A dark band at the end of the tail has already been coloured in.

Key and colours to numbered parts

1. gullet (oesophagus) (green)
2. crop (green)
3. gizzard (green)
4. intestines (green)
5. kidney (brown)
6. ovary and oviduct (yellow)
7. liver lobe (brown)
8. heart (red)
9. lungs and trachea (orange)
10. orbit (eye socket) (white)
11. brain and spinal cord—these have already been coloured black
12. skeleton of pigeon (yellow)
13. skin of pigeon (orange)

Assembly instructions

Colour the parts 1–13 using the colours suggested above. Cut out the parts and then fix into your book or onto a piece of card or paper in the following order:—

Stick down the **internal body section** towards the right hand side of your paper.

Now stick the various body organs onto the lettered, shaded areas marked on the **internal body section** in the following order:

the intestines by tab **A**
the heart by tab **B**
the liver by tab **C**
the lung by tab **D**

Now stick down the **skeleton** by its tab **E1**, over the tab **E** marked on the **internal body section**.

Stick the **skin shape** tab **E2** over tab **E1**.

Stick the **external body shape** by tab **E3** over tab **E2**. This should cover the other three parts so completing the cut out.

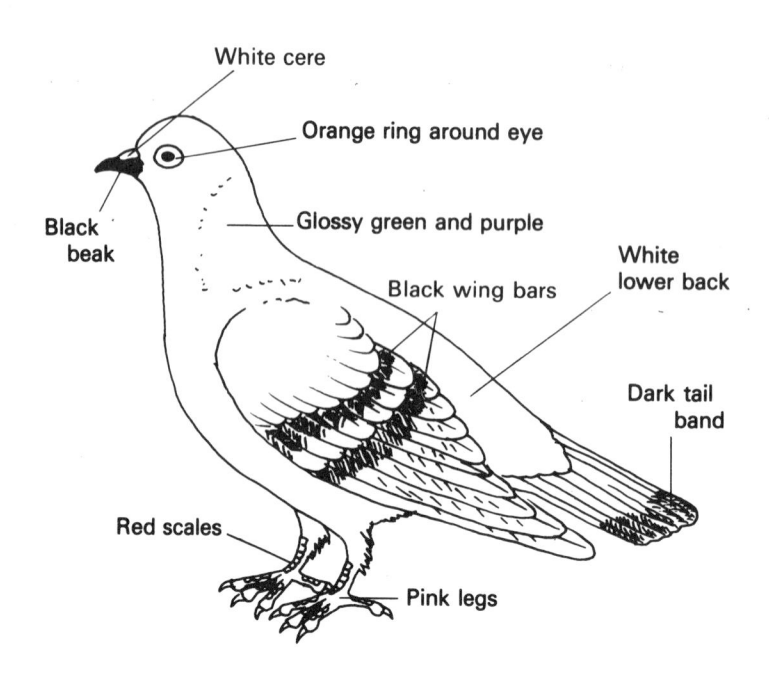

Write the title and date above the completed cut out.

Pigeon diagram labels:
- White cere
- Orange ring around eye
- Black beak
- Glossy green and purple
- Black wing bars
- White lower back
- Dark tail band
- Red scales
- Pink legs

13 Skin shape

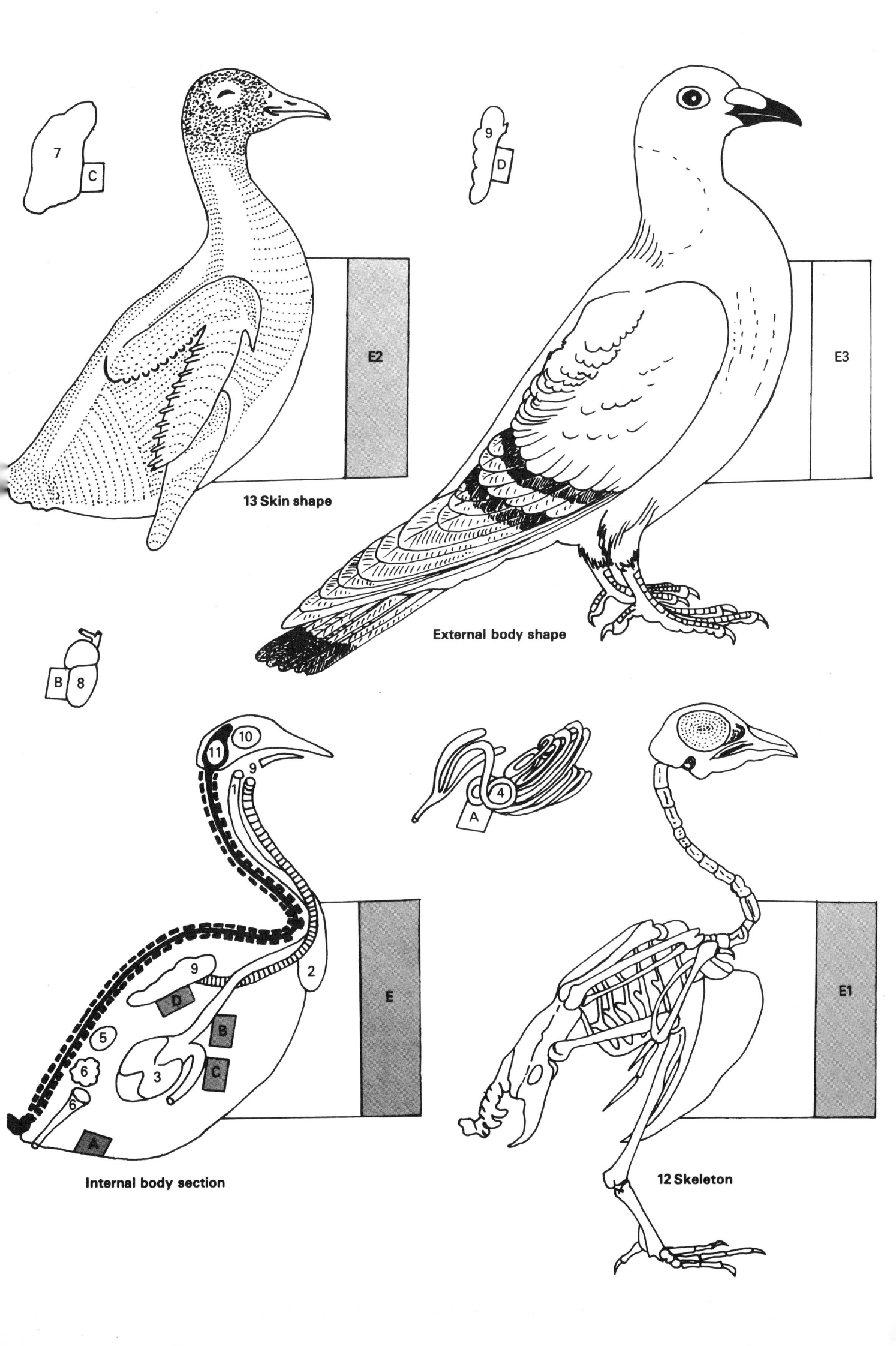

External body shape

Internal body section

12 Skeleton

Rabbit

Rabbits belong to a group of vertebrate animals called mammals. These include the monotremes, or egg-laying mammals, the marsupials, whose offspring complete their development in the mother's pouch and the placental mammals. Altogether there are over six thousand living species adapted to a very wide range of habitats including deserts, mountains, forests and the sea. They vary in shape and size from the minute shrews to the largest animal that has ever lived, the blue whale. Some, for example, the bats are able to fly. Others, such as moles, can burrow in the ground. Dolphins, whales and seals are streamlined in shape. Others, such as the giraffe with its long neck, the polar bear with its white fur and the camel with its hump have become adapted for specialised habitats.

Rabbits are grouped as mammals because they possess mammary glands which produce milk on which the young are fed. Like other mammals, they breathe air using lungs protected by a rib cage. They have a heart and circulatory system to move the food, wastes, oxygen, carbon dioxide and hormones around the body. They have a digestive system including teeth, stomach and enzymes for breaking up and liquidising the food eaten. They also have a small and large intestine for absorption of food and water. A liver stores, processes and distributes the food. Kidneys excrete the waste products formed by normal body activities.

The wild rabbit and its domesticated types of which there are several dozen including varieties such as Flemish Giants, Angoras, Sables, Chinchillas, Lopears and Himalayans are found all over the world except on a few oceanic islands. In the wild state, the rabbit normally has brown or fawn coloured fur, a small upturned tail, mobile ears and black eyes. The muzzle is characterized by the split upper lip, known as a harelip. The rabbit moves normally by unhurried loping hops. When fleeing from an enemy it puts its ears back and with its tail bobbing up and down jumps away at high speed for fifty to eighty metres before beginning to tire. Rabbits swim only if forced to and follow well trodden paths when moving from one place to another. They rest in a crouching position with their hind feet flat on the ground. They have strong blunt claws used for digging their burrows which connect together forming a warren with several openings. Rabbits spend much of the day resting underground.

Rabbits are herbivorous, feeding at night and in the early morning on crop plants, leaves and roots of weeds, bark of young trees and grass which they gnaw at using sharp, continually growing incisors. In the caecum of the rabbit the plant material is broken down by bacteria and the residue passed to the large intestine where the water is absorbed. The faeces are then passed out as dry pellets. These pellets are then eaten so that they can be redigested and the valuable food products absorbed. This process is called 'refection'.

The rabbit is an extremely timid mammal, being constantly on the alert. It has excellent hearing and sight and has good protective coloration. It is very agile and is able to make sharp changes in direction while running. This behaviour helps it to lose any animal chasing it.

The breeding season of rabbits is between February and September but young are born in all the months of the year. The female usually digs a new breeding hole and makes a nest lined with leaves, bracken and fur plucked from her body. During mating or copulation the male mounts the female from behind. After this he takes no further part in the rearing of the young. The female rabbit is viviparous, producing live young. There is a gestation period of approximately thirty days after which the babies are born. A doe has between four and eight broods in a year. The babies are born naked, blind and with closed ears. The eyes and ears open on the eleventh or twelfth day and the young can run in a fortnight. The doe has eight teats with which she suckles her young for approximately one month after which they become self-supporting. The off-spring can pair and breed after six months and they live for up to eight years.

background information

Rabbit

colour and assembly

Colour the rabbit's **external body shape** brown or grey brown and the visible inside of the ear pink or pinky grey. Leave the belly white.

Key and colours to numbered parts

1 gullet (oesophagus) (green)
2 stomach (green)
3 duodenum (green)
4 small intestine (ileum and jejunum) (green)
5 caecum and appendix (green)
6 large intestine (colon) (green)
7 rectum and anus (green)
8 pancreas (yellow)
9 spleen (red)
10 kidneys (brown)
11 ureter (duct from the kidney leading to the bladder) (yellow)
12 bladder (yellow)
13 ovaries (yellow)
14 uterus (2 in rabbits) (yellow)
15 vagina (yellow)
16 liver (brown)
17 gall bladder (green)
18 windpipe (trachea) (orange)
19 lungs (orange)
20 heart (red)
21 diaphragm (red)
22 brain and spinal cord—these have already been coloured black

Assembly instructions

Colour the parts **1–22** using the colours suggested above. Cut out the parts and fix them onto a piece of card or paper in the following order:—

Stick down the **internal body section** in the centre of the paper.

Now stick the various body organs onto the lettered, shaded areas marked on the **internal body section** in the following order:

the heart by tab **A**
the small intestine by tab **B1** over the area marked **B**
the lung by tab **C**
the liver by tab **D**
the large intestine by tab **B2** over tab **B1**
the female reproductive organ by tab **E**
the skeleton by tab **F**

Carefully line up the **external body shape** so that it covers all the **internal body section**.

Now stick it down by its tab and bend back along the dotted line.

Write the title and date above the completed cut out.

Skeleton

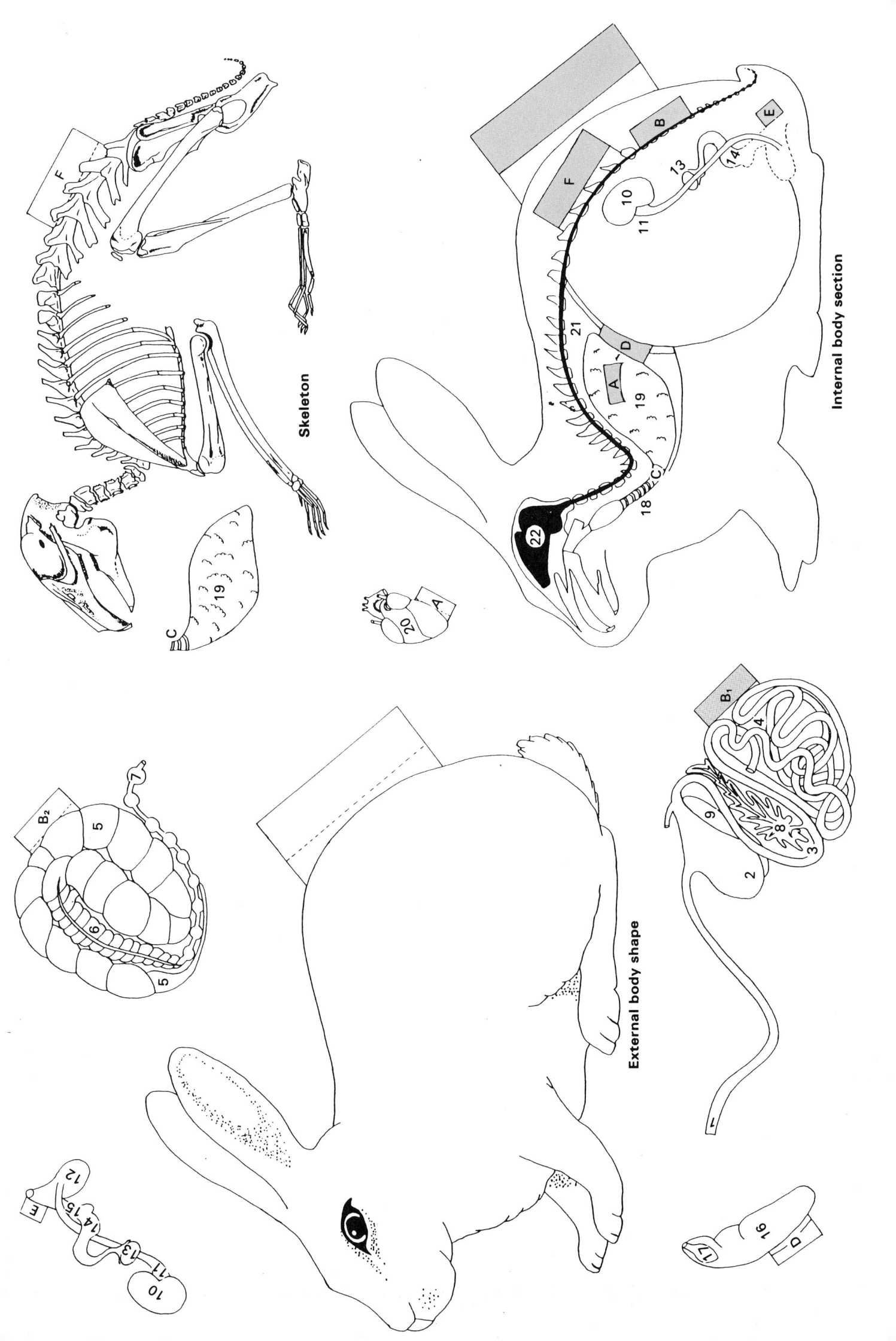

Internal body section

External body shape

Earthworm

Earthworms belong to a group of invertebrate animals called annelids. Annelids have long, cylindrical bodies divided into many small segments or rings. Many animals in this group are brightly coloured and some marine species are amongst the most beautiful animals living in the sea. The group includes the lugworms and ragworms used as bait by fishermen, the beautifully coloured peacock fan worms as well as the earthworms in the soil and blood sucking leeches. Earthworms vary enormously in size. Some specimens are only a few millimetres long while certain tropical species grow to a length of three or four metres.

Earthworms have a fairly simple internal body structure. There is a simple nervous system running the length of the body and this has individual nerves running to each segment. The digestive system is also simple in structure and it is designed to deal with large quantities of soil. Earthworms have a blood system and the outer skin contains a rich supply of blood vessels which help in breathing. The earthworm takes in oxygen and loses carbon dioxide through its moist skin.

Earthworms prefer soils which do not dry out, which are not too acid and which are rich in humus. They are found in large numbers and some estimates suggest a population of one million worms to the hectare is not unusual. In some grassland areas counts of more than three million worms per hectare have been made.

Earthworms burrow, partly by pushing soil aside and partly by swallowing it. The burrows are lined by a kind of cement made by earth which has passed through the worm's body. Most earthworms stay within one metre of the surface of the soil although quite deep burrows are made in cold weather, when the worms seek warmth and in hot weather when they try to avoid drying out.

Earthworms normally stay in their burrows during the day but at night they come out to gather fallen leaves, either leaving the burrow completely or with their tails anchored in the entrance. As an earthworm burrows, the soil it swallows passes through its gut where the various nutrients are taken out and absorbed into the body. The undigested soil particles pass out of the body through the anus. Earthworms move partly by muscular contractions which alter the width and length of the body and partly by means of fine bristles called chaetae sticking out of the body wall.

Earthworms have no eyes but they can detect changes in light intensity by means of sensitive nerve endings in the skin. They can also respond to vibrations in the ground as well as chemical and temperature changes in their surroundings. Earthworms have numerous predators including frogs, toads, birds of various kinds, moles and shrews.

Earthworms have both male and female organs in the same body and are, therefore, called hermaphrodite. They usually mate at night in warm weather. They lie side by side with their ends still in the burrows, the two bodies being held together by slime produced by special cells in the wall of the clitellum or 'saddle'. In this position they exchange sperms over a period of three to four hours. Egg laying begins about a day or so after mating and it continues for several months. As the eggs are released, they pass into a band or girdle of material produced by the clitellum. When this band is fully formed, the worm gradually draws backwards and slips the band enclosing the eggs over its head, just as we would take off a sweater. As the band containing the eggs slips over the worm's head the two ends close up forming a cocoon. This protects the eggs inside and prevents them from drying out.

An individual earthworm will produce many cocoons in a breeding season. Usually only one of the eggs in each cocoon develops into a young worm and this process often takes as long as five months. Once it has hatched from the cocoon the young worm starts to feed and grow quite quickly and after a year it becomes sexually mature.

Earthworm

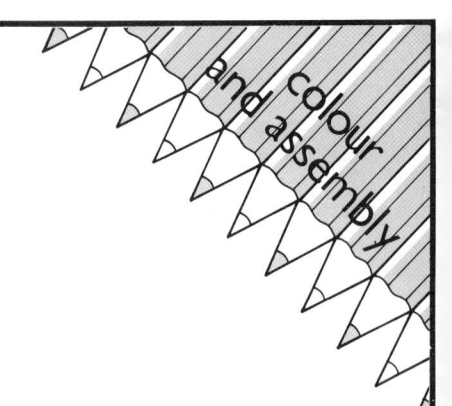

colour and assembly

Colour the segments on the **external body shape** pink.

Key and colours to numbered parts

1. cerebral ganglion and nerve ring—these have already been coloured black
2. nerve cord—these have already been coloured black
3. buccal cavity (green)
4. pharynx (green)
5. muscle strands (red)
6. oesophagus (green)
7. 5 pairs of pseudo hearts (red)
8. dorsal blood vessel and segmental blood vessels (red)
9. crop (green)
10. gizzard (green)
11. intestine (green)
12. nephridia (brown)
13. seminal vesicles including testes and vas deferens (yellow)
14. spermotheca (yellow)
15. ovary (yellow)
16. oviduct (yellow)
17. outer (muscular) body wall (pink)
18. clitellum (saddle) (orange)
19. anus (green)

Assembly instructions

Colour the parts labelled 1–19 using the colours suggested above. Cut out the parts and fix them onto a piece of card or paper in the following order:—

Fix down the **internal body section 1**, except for tab **D** which should be left unglued, in the middle of the page.

Now stick the various body organs onto the lettered, shaded areas marked on the **internal body section 1** in the following order:

The seminal vesicles (13) by tab **B**. Place some glue onto the area marked **B** and fix section **B₁** onto it.

The cerebral ganglion (1) by tab **A** having cut out the white centre portion before hand so forming a nerve ring.

The alimentary canal section by putting glue on the shaded area marked **C** on the **internal body section 1** and fixing the alimentary canal onto it and so covering area **C**. Now slide the buccal cavity (3) end through the nerve ring. This will hold it in place at the anterior or head end.

Take the **external body shape** and turn it over so that you can see the white side and stick its tab **D-D** on the **internal body section 1**. Now take **internal body section 2** and fix it, facing upwards, onto the **external body shape** in such a way that the gut and nephridia (12) match up where they meet on **internal body section 1**.

Allow glue to dry and then carefully bend tab **D** upwards and over so that the **external body shape** covers the **internal body section 1** completely. They should match up exactly if you have glued the parts together correctly.

Write the title and date above the completed cut-out.

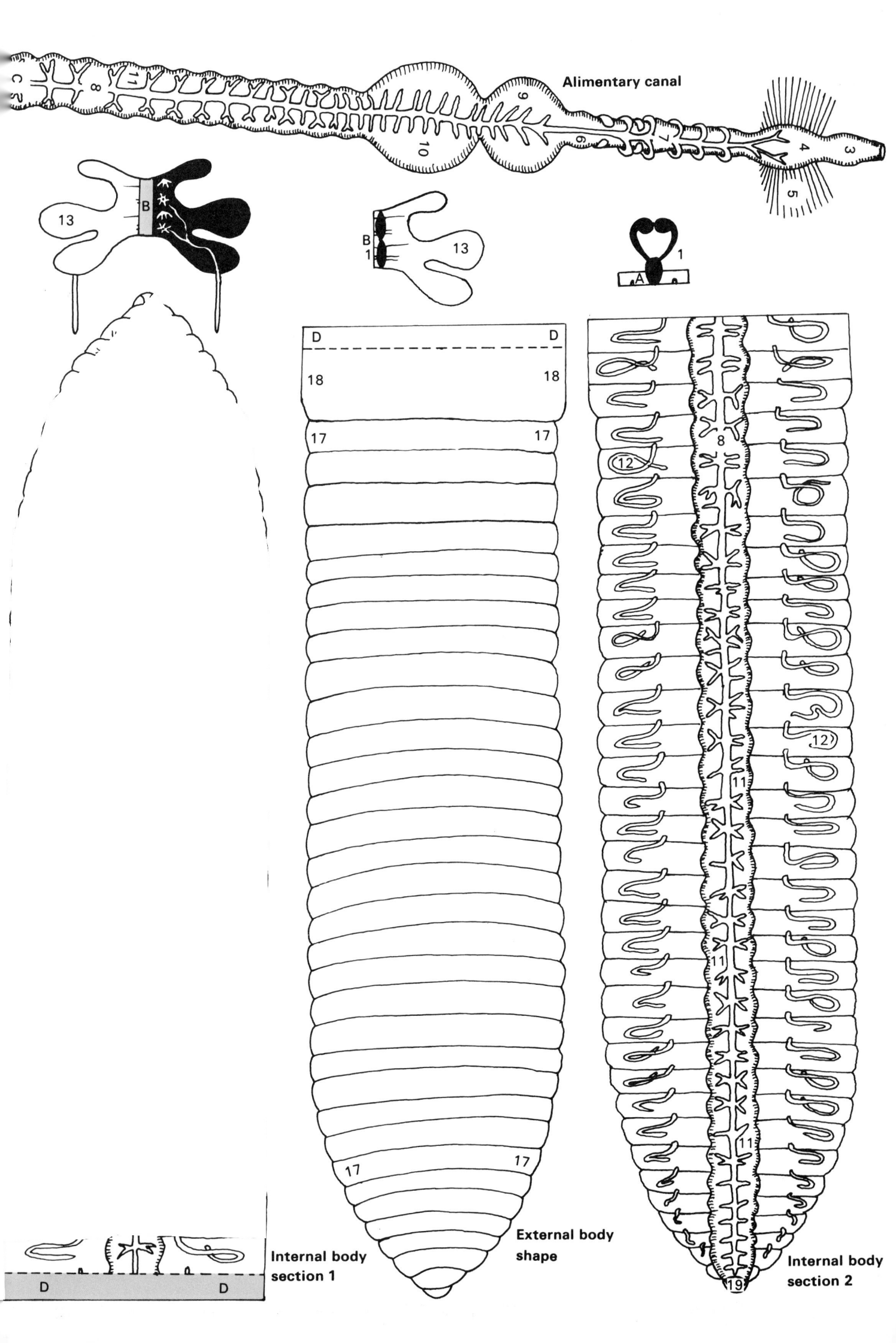

Alimentary canal

Internal body section 1

External body shape

Internal body section 2

Spider

Spiders belong to a large group of animals called the arachnids which is one of the groups making up the arthropods. There are more than fifty thousand different species of spider living in various parts of the world. These range in size from the giant bird-eating spiders found in South America to the world's smallest spider found in Samoa which is no bigger than the full stop at the end of this sentence.

Spiders have a characteristic structure in which the body is divided into two main parts, unlike insects which have a head, thorax and abdomen. In spiders the head and thorax are joined to form one structure and the abdomen is attached behind. All spiders have four pairs of legs attached to the first part of the body and they have a varying number of eyes on the head. However, unlike insects, spiders do not have antennae. The mouth is generally small and it is used for sucking the body juices from other animals. It is surrounded by a pair of jaws or pincers and, in some spiders, these are specially enlarged for catching and killing other animals. Other spiders rely more on the technique of setting various kinds of traps in order to catch their prey. Some species even resort to subterfuge in the form of camouflage, trapdoors or pits in order to obtain food.

Just behind the spiders 'waist', on each side of the undersurface, are a pair of slits which open into a body chamber containing the breathing apparatus. Spiders breathe atmospheric air and their lungs are made of delicate, thin plates arranged like the pages of a book.

At the end of the spider's body are special organs called spinnerets. These produce the thin, silk strands used to make their webs, to manufacture snares, homes, cocoons for eggs and even for transport.

Not all spiders make webs and those that do use different building techniques. One of the common methods of web construction involves the spider spinning threads to form the radii of a circle. These initial threads are attached to anything in the surroundings after which a circumference thread is added. When this has been done, the spider spins a spiral thread starting from the centre and working out towards the circumference. When this is complete the spider then spins a second thread but this time starting from the circumference and working inwards. It attaches this thread to each radius in turn and as it does this, it removes the first spiral which acted only as a scaffold from which to build the second. The web is used to trap other insects and the spider has a special communication cord running from the centre to where it is hiding somewhere on the edge of the web. When this line is triggered off, the spider rushes out and captures its prey. As the spider bites the animal it injects a paralysing poison after which the victim is rolled up in a gossamer 'blanket' and carried off to the spider's 'larder' to be sucked dry at a later stage or, in some cases, to be stored.

Mating in spiders is a fascinating process. The male spider is usually smaller than the female and he is also different in having a swollen 'boxing glove' tip to each palp. This acts as a reservoir for sperm and it has to be recharged after each mating. When the male spider comes in contact with the female he inserts his swollen palps into the female's reproductive opening and once these are locked in he pumps sperm into the female's body. This is stored for later use. Sometimes the female eats the male after mating but this is quite a rare occurrence although it always happens in the case of the Black Widow spider.

Once the eggs have been fertilised, several hundred are laid in a cocoon of silk which is placed near the 'larder'. When the young spiders hatch out there is a meal ready and waiting. The young spiders of some species use silk strands called gossamer threads as a form of parachute, being lifted in the warm summer air currents from one place to another. They may be transported only a few metres from where they were born but on other occasions the air currents may carry them several kilometres.

Spider

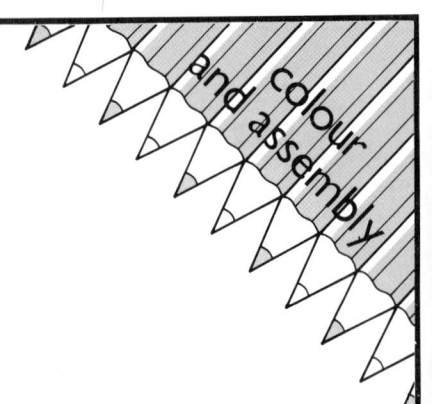

colour and assembly

Colour the **external body shape** brown.

Key and colours to numbered parts

1. mouth (green)
2. oesophagus (green)
3. sucking stomach (green) with muscles (red)
4. caecum (digestive gland) (green)
5. intestine (green)
6. malpighian (kidney) tubule (brown)
7. rectal caecum (green)
8. rectum (green)
9. anus (green)
10. digestive gland (liver) (brown)
11. lung book (orange)
12. heart (red)
13. silk glands (blue)
14. spinnerets (blue)
15. ovary (yellow)
16. brain—this has already been coloured black
17. eyes
18. poison gland (blue)
19. walking legs (brown)
20. pedipalps (brown)

Assembly instructions

Colour the parts labelled **1–20** using the colours suggested above. Cut out the parts and fix them onto a piece of card or paper in the following order:—

Stick down the **internal body section** in the centre of your paper, leaving the legs and pedipalp free and unstuck.

Now stick the various body organs onto the lettered, shaded areas marked on the **internal body section** in the following order:

the brain (**16**) and the eyes (**17**) by tab **B**

the alimentary canal by tab **A** and **D** (at the same time slip the oesophagus under the brain)

the heart (**12**) by tab **C**

the lung book (**11**) by tab **F** on the heart

the ovary (**15**) by tab **E**

Now stick the **external body shape** by tab **G** onto the lettered, shaded area marked **G** on the **internal body section** so that all the organs are covered.

Write the title and date above the completed cut out.

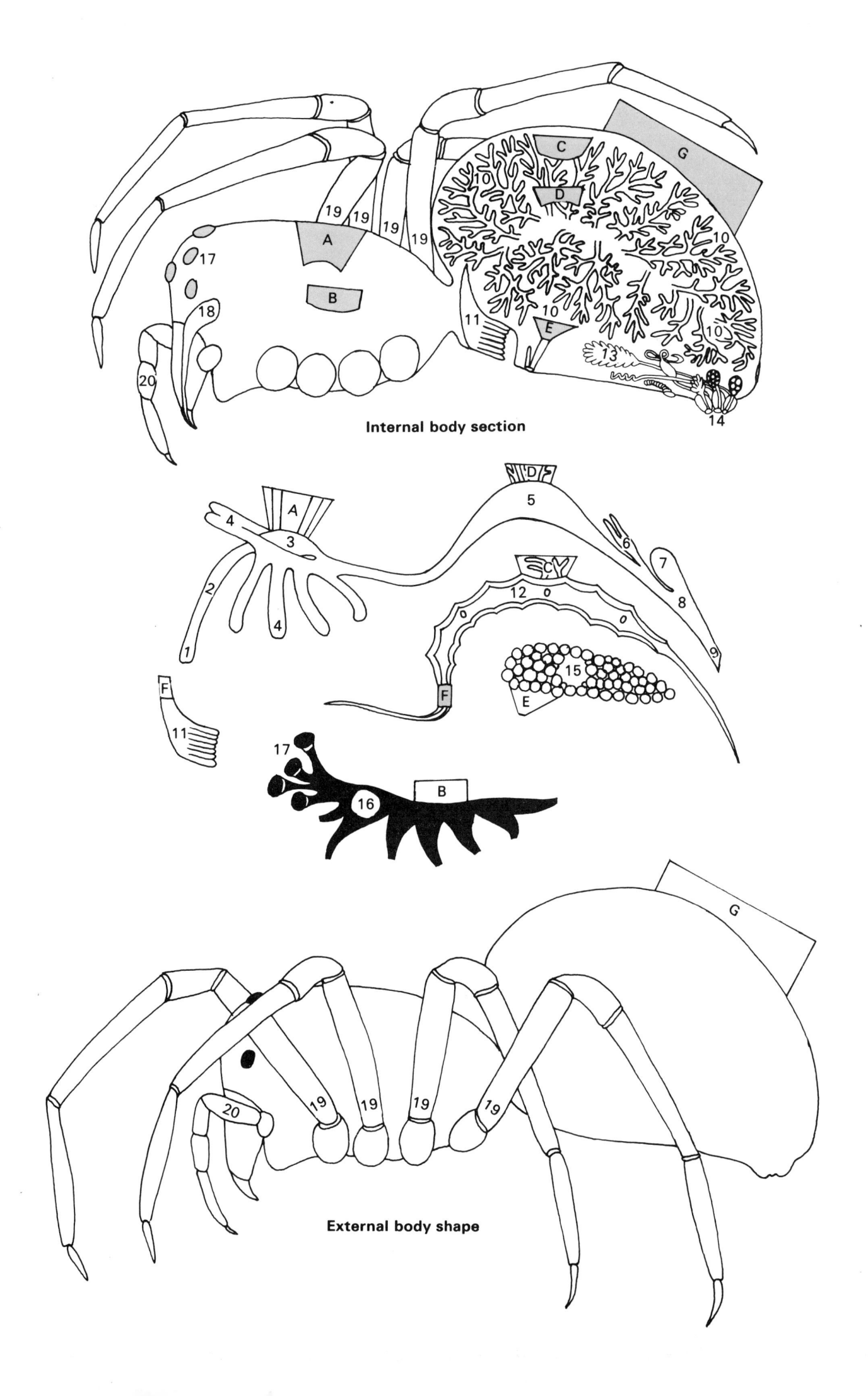

Internal body section

External body shape

Starfish

Starfish belong to a group of animals called echinoderms of which there are over five and a half thousand known species. Apart from starfish, this group also includes cushion stars, brittle stars, sea urchins, sea cucumbers, sea lilies and feather-stars. All echinoderms have spiny skins, tube feet and a body plan based on the number five. They all live in the sea and are found in shallow coastal waters as well as on the sea bed at depths up to six hundred metres.

Starfish are often brightly coloured with reds and oranges and some species are amongst the most beautiful of marine animals. They tend not to be camouflaged but instead rely on sea weed and rock crevices in which to cover or conceal themselves. The star-shaped body has a chalky outer skeleton made up of plates bound together by muscles and other tissue. The spines, so well developed in the sea urchins, are short and blunt. On the upper surface of the starfish is a sieve-like plate called the madreporite which allows water to enter and leave the internal water system. There is also an anal opening from the digestive system. On the under surface there is a round, central mouth and five grooves, each one running out along one of the arms. Each groove has four rows of tube feet extending from it. These structures are used for breathing, movement and feeding.

Starfish live on sandy bottoms, in rock pools and in crevices on rocky shores. They have a well developed sense of touch and they use this to find shellfish and other animals on which they feed. When a starfish has found an animal such as a mussel it wraps its arms around it and starts to pull. Eventually it overcomes the resistance of the mussel and slowly forces the two halves of the shell apart. The starfish now inserts its stomach, which can be turned inside out, through its mouth opening and produces digestive juices which slowly weaken and finally kill its prey. The digested food is stored in special glands in the digestive system which act as a kind of 'liver'.

Starfish walk by means of the tube feet which act in a co-ordinated way. By using its feet in this way the animal moves forward very slowly at a speed of about fifteen centimetres a minute. Although starfish seem to lack a well developed nervous system they do have a number of major nerves including some connected to the tube feet. This makes the feet sensitive to touch. There are also some small tentacles and a light sensitive eyespot at the tip of each arm.

Starfish are able to grow new parts when old ones are damaged or lost. This is useful in an animal which cannot escape easily from enemies and danger. A single arm with part of the main body will grow a completely new body. In all species, arms which have broken off anywhere along their length are regenerated, although this takes time. In fact if an arm is injured, it is often cast off near the base. This process is called autonomy and is a protective device.

Starfish are unisexual, each individual possessing either ovaries or testis. The female starfish can release as many as two and a half million eggs in a two hour period and biologists have estimated that as many as two hundred million eggs may be produced in a single breeding season. A male produces many times this number of sperm. The eggs and sperm are liberated into the sea during the spring and fertilisation occurs at random. The microscopic larvae swim in the surface plankton for several weeks while feeding on diatoms. They grow very quickly soon taking on the shape of the adult and sinking to the sea bottom where they grow, becoming sexually mature after only one year's growth.

background information

Starfish

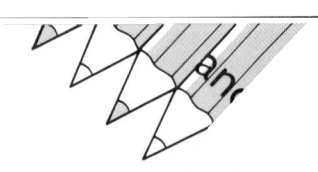

Colour the **external body shape** orange leaving the circles, squares, 1, 7 and 14 white.

Key and colours to numbered parts

1. eye spot (white)
2. mouth (pale green)
3. stomach (pale green)
4. digestive gland (caecum) (green)
5. rectal gland (pale green)
6. rectum (pale green)
7. anus (pale green)
8. gonads (female or male) (yellow)
9. tube feet (pale blue)
10. ampullae (pale blue)
11. water vascular ring (pale blue)
12. tiedemann's bodies (pale blue)
13. stone canal (pale blue)
14. madreporite (pale blue)
15. ossicles (white)
16. spines (white)
17. upper (aboral) surface (orange)

Assembly instructions

Colour the parts labelled 1–17 using the colours suggested above. Cut out the parts and fix them onto a piece of card or paper in the following order:—

Stick down the **external body shape** (lower surface) in the centre of the page by its tab **A** only, so that the tube feet face downwards. On top of it and facing upwards, so that you can see the organs, stick the **internal body section** lining both up. You will find that tab **B** on the **internal body section** will lie above the tab **A** position on the **external body shape** (lower surface).

Now fix the gonads (**8**) onto the numbered, marked areas on the **internal body section**.

Cover the area marked **B** on the **internal body section** with glue and then lower the digestive system onto it facing upwards so that tab **C** lies above tab **B** and facing upwards.

Lastly, cover the area marked **C** with glue and again lining up the **external body shape** so that the arm with a line across it is above tab **C** on the digestive system, fix the **external body shape** (upper surface) down. The **external body shape** should cover the rest of the starfish completely.

Write the title and date above the completed cut out.

External body shape (lower surface)

External body shape (upper surface)

Gonads

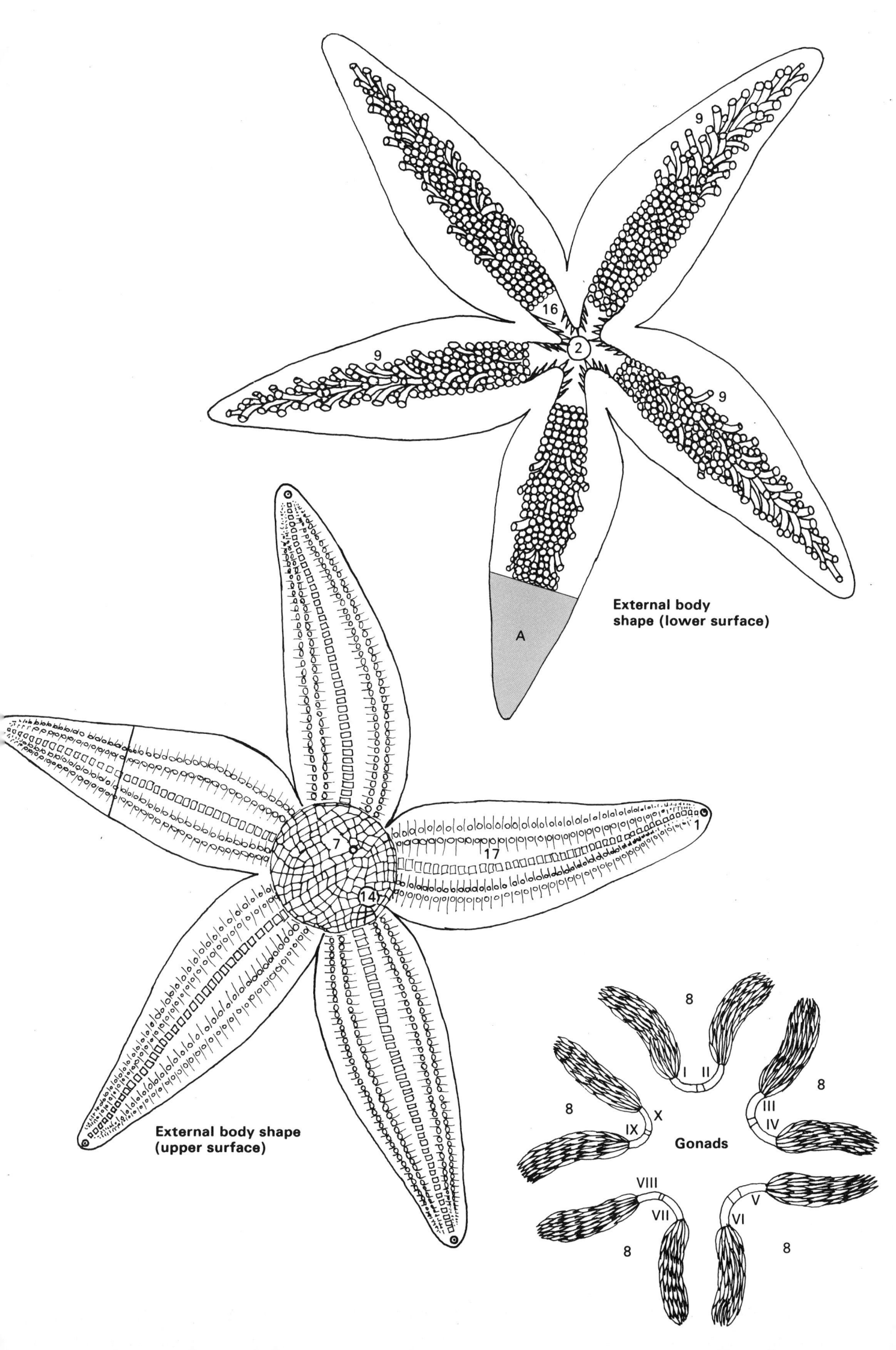

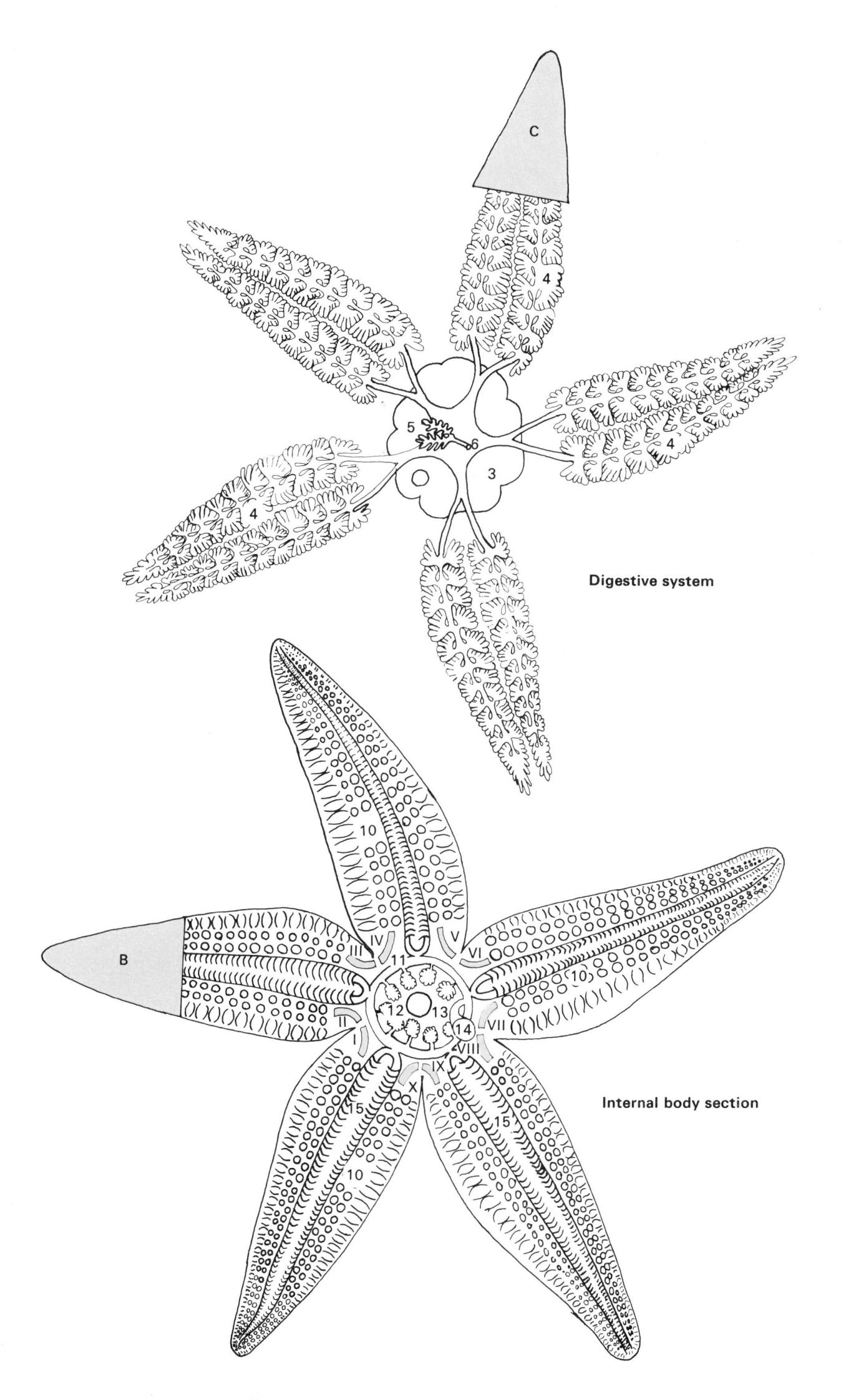

Digestive system

Internal body section

Butterfly

background information

Insects are members of a large group of animals called arthropods, which means 'jointed limbed' animals. This group contains many familiar animals including crabs, spiders, butterflies and moths. There are many different kinds of insect on the earth's surface and biologists have estimated that there are more than one million different species. Some species of insect are very numerous. For example, a single termite colony in the tropics may contain as many as two hundred million individual animals. Within the insect group there are probably about one hundred thousand different kinds of butterfly and moth and it is likely that there are still many species not yet discovered.

All butterflies have a similar structure. The adult body is divided into three parts, head, thorax and abdomen. The head has a pair of compound eyes for seeing and a pair of long, thin antennae used for smelling and feeling. It also contains a coiled, tubular proboscis which is used for sucking plant juices and nectar. Some butterflies suck the sugary juices from rotten and decaying fruit and even the sap exuding from the bark of trees.

The adult butterfly has three pairs of legs attached to the thorax and two pairs of wings. The wings are covered with tiny scales which are often very brightly coloured. These colours are characteristic for any one species, although there are always slight variations. In some species of butterfly the colours are arranged on the hindwings as large eye-spots which are displayed to frighten off an attacker. For example the Peacock butterfly is able to escape predators in this way.

The size of the body and wings vary from one species to another. The smallest butterfly has a wing span of only a few millimetres while some of the Birdwings, which live on the island of Papua New Guinea, have a wing span greater than 25 centimetres. These butterflies get their name from their enormous size, many of them are larger than some of the birds which live in the same forest areas. In some species the males and females are different in size, shape and colour. This is true, for example, in the Birdwings where the females are very much bigger than the males but much less colourful.

Butterflies breathe through a system of microscopic tubes called trachea which run from the outside of the body to the organs inside. Oxygen passes down these tubes to reach all the body parts requiring it and carbon dioxide, produced by the body cells passes up from inside the body to the outside atmosphere. A butterfly has a simple blood system and a nervous system which runs down the length of the body. It has a simple excretory kidney made up of malpighian tubules.

Butterflies have a characteristic life which is made up of four main stages. After the adults have mated, and this frequently happens during flight, the female lays her eggs. Many butterflies lay their eggs on a particular species of plant because the caterpillars which hatch from the eggs will feed on no other type of vegetation. This means that the distribution of different types of butterfly is often associated with particular plants and where they grow. The caterpillar is the main feeding stage of the butterfly's life cycle. Food is devoured very quickly and the caterpillar soon grows to full size. It does this by shedding its outer skin at regular intervals, a process known as moulting. Once it has done this it turns into a pupa or chrysalis. Within the pupal skin a series of complex chemical changes take place, called metamorphosis, and eventually, after several weeks, the adult butterfly emerges. The time taken to complete metamorphosis varies depending on the species and in some cases butterflies living in colder climates may stay in the chrysalis form throughout the winter. The adult butterfly may live for many months but in some tropical species it survives only a few days during which time it is able to complete the mating process so that the species continues.

Butterfly

Colour the lower surface of the right hand wings brown. Colour the upper surface of both wings using the photograph on the cover of this book as a guide.

Key and colours to numbered parts

1. internal body section and nervous system (no colour needed)
2. internal body section and circulatory system
3. oesophagus (green)
4. crop (green)
5. stomach and gizzard (green)
6. intestine (green)
7. malpighian tubules (kidney) (brown)
8. rectum and anus (green)
9. heart and aorta (light red)
10. muscles (dark red)
11. antenna (dark brown with yellow tip)
12. compound eye (blue-/green/purple)
13. reproductive system (yellow)
14. abdomen (light brown)
15. thorax (brown with orange hairs)
16. head (brown)
17. tracheal system (orange)
18. coiled proboscis (orange)
19. hind leg ⎫
20. middle leg ⎬ (dark brown)
21. fore leg ⎭

Assembly instructions

Colour the parts 1–21 using the colours suggested above. Cut out the parts and fix them onto a piece of card or paper in the following order:—

Stick down the **internal body section and nervous system (1)** on the right hand side of the paper leaving a margin of 5 cm. Fix down the whole of **left hand wings** (upper surface) so that tab **H** fits into the space left in the wings.

Now stick the various body organs onto the lettered, shaded areas marked on the **internal body section and nervous system** in the following order:—

reproductive system by tab **A**
digestive system by tab **B**
tracheal system by tab **C**

Take the **external body shape and lower surface of right hand wings** and cut the head, thorax and abdomen in half along the line drawn. Now carefully glue the **lower surface of the right hand wings** and the half body to the **external body shape and right hand wings (upper surface)** so that they line up exactly. At the same time fix together the two sides of the antennae (11). Take this completed piece of the butterfly and fold the head, thorax and abdomen in half and back.

Now fix the **internal body section and circulatory system (2)** onto the remaining bare surface left on the **external body shape and right hand wings (upper surface)**. This will leave half of the **internal body section and circulatory system** and the tab on the **external body shape and right hand wings (upper surface)** still free. Fix the half piece cut off the **external body shape and lower surface of the right hand wings** onto this bare half left over.

Fix the proboscis by its tab **D** onto the shaded area **D**. At this point the **external body shape and lower surface of the right hand wings** should look complete again. Fix this completed body section and wings by its free tab over the shaded area tab **H**.

Fold the wings back so that you can only see the **lower surface of the right hand wings and body**. Fix the legs onto shaded areas marked **E, F, G** so letters cover letters and then the single antenna (11) onto the paper under and in line with the free antenna so that when you open the butterfly out, exposing both the upper wing surfaces, it has two antennae in the normal way.

Write the title and date above the completed cut out.

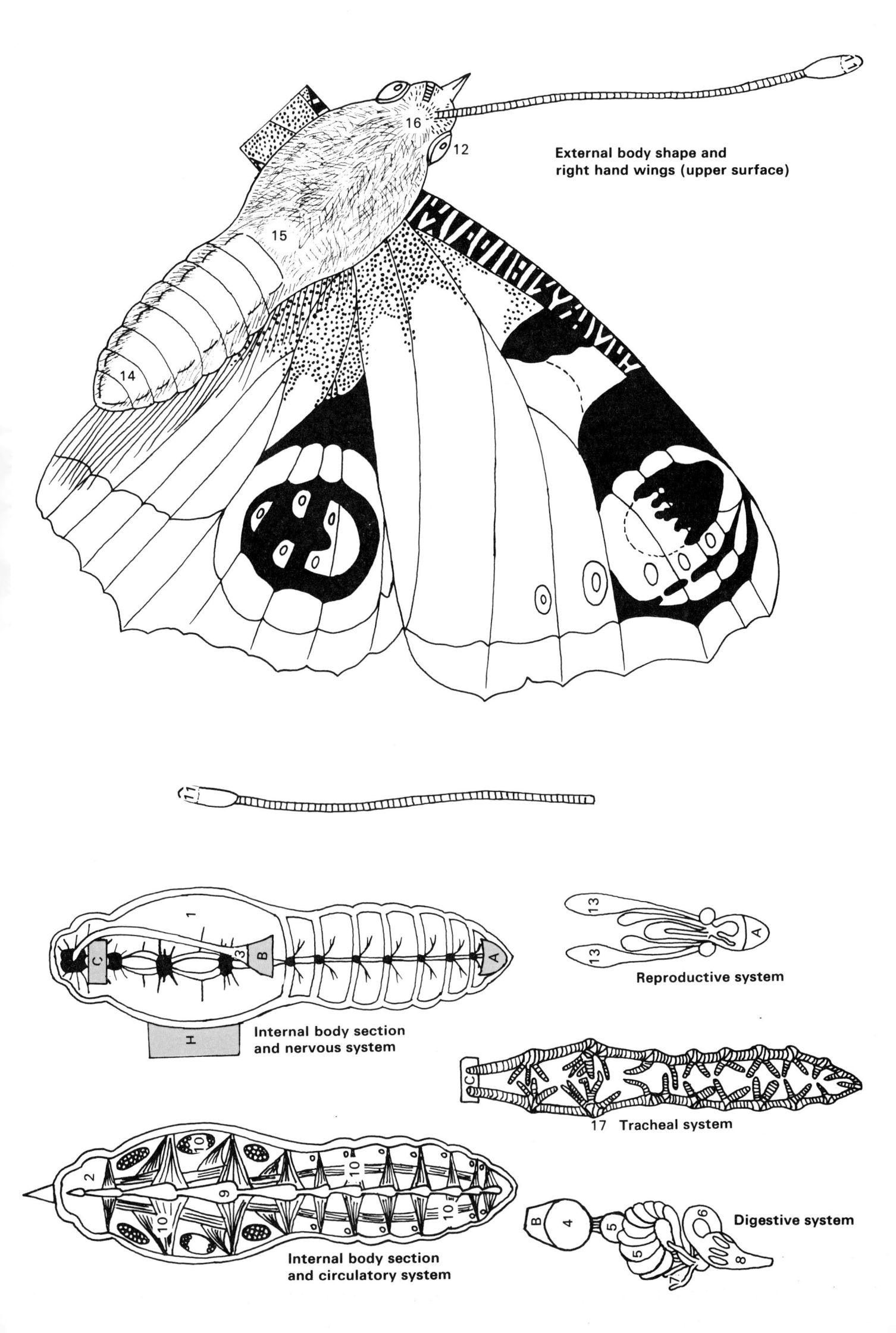

External body shape and right hand wings (upper surface)

Internal body section and nervous system

Reproductive system

17 Tracheal system

Internal body section and circulatory system

Digestive system

Left hand wings (upper surface)

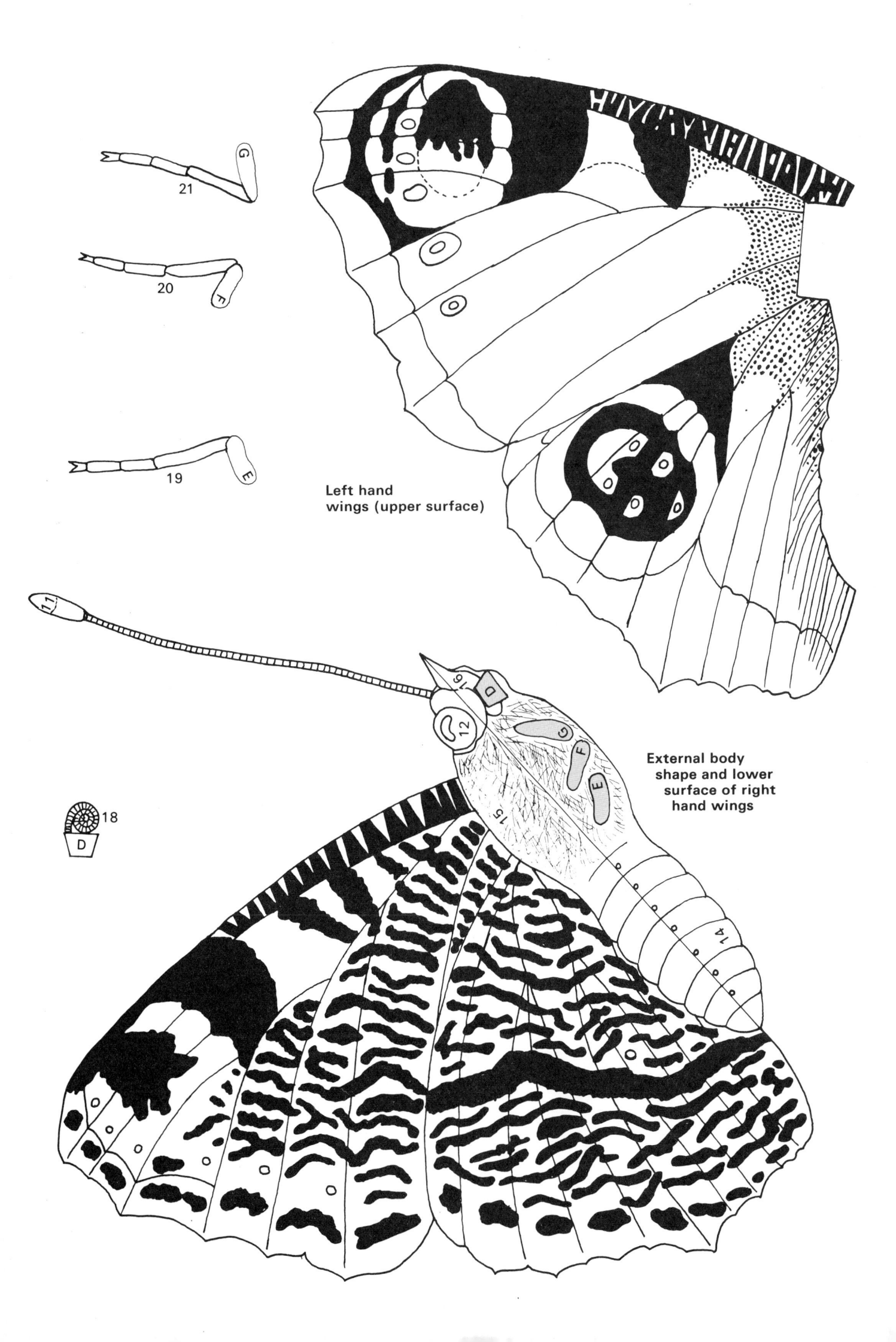

External body shape and lower surface of right hand wings

Snail

background information

Snails belong to a group of animals called molluscs. The word mollusc means 'soft-bodied'. Soft-bodied may seem at first sight a curious name for animals which often have a hard shell. This name was first used by the French naturalist Cuvier in 1798 for the cuttlefish, octopus and squids which either have an internal shell or none at all. Since then the name has come to cover both shelled and non-shelled forms. Biologists have identified more than one hundred thousand different species of mollusc living in a wide variety of habitats from the tops of mountains to the sea bed many hundreds of metres below the surface.

Molluscs include animals such as clams, cockles, mussels, octopuses, oysters, squids, whelks and winkles. They come in all shapes and sizes ranging from the Giant Clam of the great Barrier Reef to the smallest mollusc, *Ammonicera rota,* which is the size of a pin-head. Snails have got a name for sluggishness and many bivalves, such as mussels are fixed permanently on the sea, lake or river bed making them easy prey for predators. However, some molluscs, such as the squids, have become powerful predators themselves. Other species have evolved successful methods of protection. The Geography Cone shell can produce a fatal sting while Cuttle fish are capable of laying down a 'smoke screen' under the cover of which they make their escape. Within the main group, one of the largest subgroups is the gastropods which include slugs and snails as well as the tropical conchs of the Caribbean, the giant trumpet shells of the Indian and Pacific oceans and the beautiful cowrie shells found on many tropical coral reefs.

The snail's body is divided into a head, foot and hump in which most of the body organs are found. The body has a rough texture due to a large number of small grooves running along its length. The head carries four tentacles, the short ones being sensitive to touch and smell and the long ones to light.

Snails move on a large, flat, slimy foot which is thrown into a series of minute ripples or waves by muscles in its wall. They breathe through a small hole leading to the mantle cavity which acts like a lung. The mantle also produces the shell. The mouth is a small slit on the underside of the head in which there is a single, black, hard upper jaw and a long tongue or radula. The radula is covered with microscopic, sharp teeth. It works like a conveyer belt, rasping away at pieces of vegetation which make up the snail's diet.

Snails are found in a wide variety of habitats but they prefer moist conditions and are active mainly at night. They tend to have a well developed 'homing instinct' and are extremely gregarious, often roosting in large numbers under stones or in cracks in walls. In very hot conditions they aestivate by producing a thin seal across the entrance to the shell. This protects the animal inside from excessive heat and water loss while, at the same time, allowing it to breathe. In hot climates a number of snails climb up fence posts, tree trunks and dried flower stems in order to keep cool during the summer.

Snails are hermaphrodite, having both male and female sex organs in the same body. They produce sperm for most of the year but eggs for a short period of time only. In the case of snails living in temperate countries, this tends to be in the summer. The garden snail shows complex courtship before copulation and this includes the shooting of 'love darts' at one another. After fertilisation, each snail lays between forty and a hundred eggs in a moist hole in the ground. Each egg is a transparent structure about three millimetres in diameter. After several weeks, tiny snails hatch and begin to feed. They gradually grow into adult snails which live for a period of five to six years.

Snail

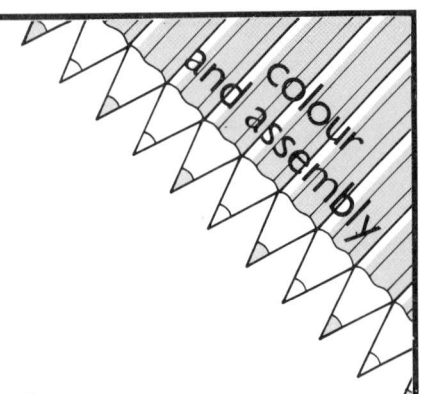

colour and assembly

Key and colours to numbered parts

1. large tentacles with eyes (pale yellow)
2. genital pore (white)
3. foot (pale yellow)
4. external shell (body, spine and apex) (mottled brown and yellow)
5. whorls (pale grey)
6. lip and columella (white)
7. mantle collar (white)
8. mantle (pale green)
9. respiratory pore (white)
10. heart (red)
11. kidney (nephridium) (brown)
12. body wall (pale yellow)
13. liver (dark brown)
14. albumen gland (white)
15. ovo-testis or hermaphrodite gland (yellow)
16. pulmonary chamber (pale green)
17. blood vessels (red)
18. ureter (yellow)
19. radula and horny jaw plate (yellow)
20. salivary glands and ducts (white)
21. oesophagus (green)
22. crop (green)
23. intestine (green)
24. cerebral ganglion and nerves—these are already coloured black
25. retractor muscle of foot (red)
26. penis and ducts (yellow)
27. vagina and oviduct (yellow)
28. dart sac (yellow)
29. mucous gland (white)
30. sperm sac and ducts (yellow)

Assembly instructions

Colour the parts 1–30 using the colours suggested above. Cut out the parts and fix them onto a piece of card or paper in the following order:—

Stick down the **internal body section (a)** a little below the centre of the page.

Now take **internal body section (b)** and fold along the dotted lines so that the bottom part, which includes numbers **12**, **13** and **23**, lies under the round mantle section on the right hand side of the section. Take the free **mantle section** and fix it onto the back of the mantle section on the **internal body section (b)** so that it lines up with the fold line. Fix on the radula (**19**) by its tab **B** to the shaded area marked **B**.

Take the reproductive organs and bend along the dotted lines. Now fix this section down onto the position marked **D** on the **internal body section (b)**.

Keeping the organs folded up, fix the **internal body section (b)** in the space in the **internal body section (a)**. They should line up exactly when glued down.

Stick the **inside of the shell section** on the back of the **external shell** so that they line up on one another.

Fix the shell by its tab **A** onto the shaded area marked **A** on the **internal body section (a)** so that it covers the body parts and then fix the **part of the body wall** by its tab **C** on the place marked **C** on the **internal body section (b)**.

If everything has been done correctly then no internal organs can be seen and only the external features of the snail should be visible.

Write the title and date above the completed cut out.

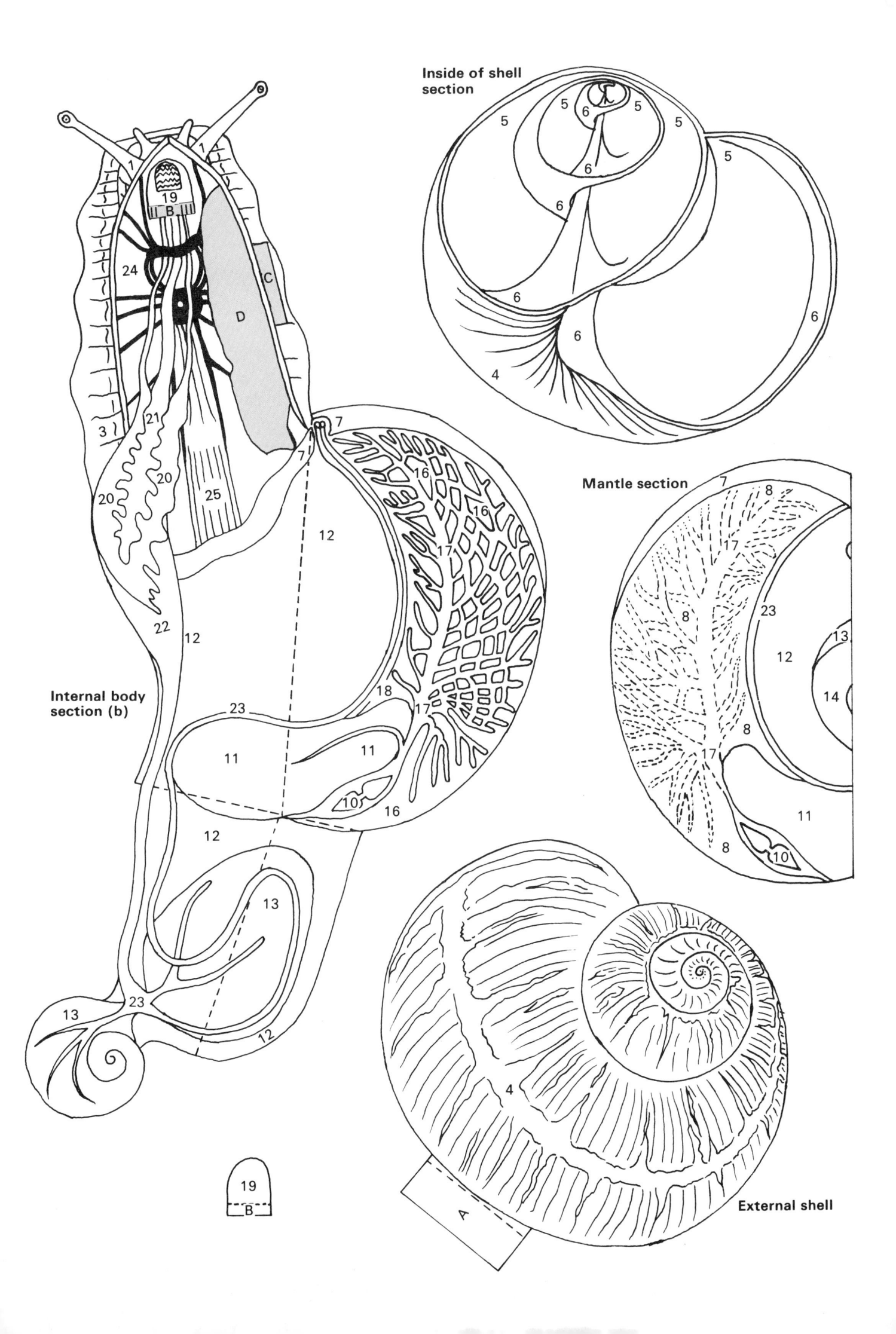

Inside of shell section

Mantle section

Internal body section (b)

External shell

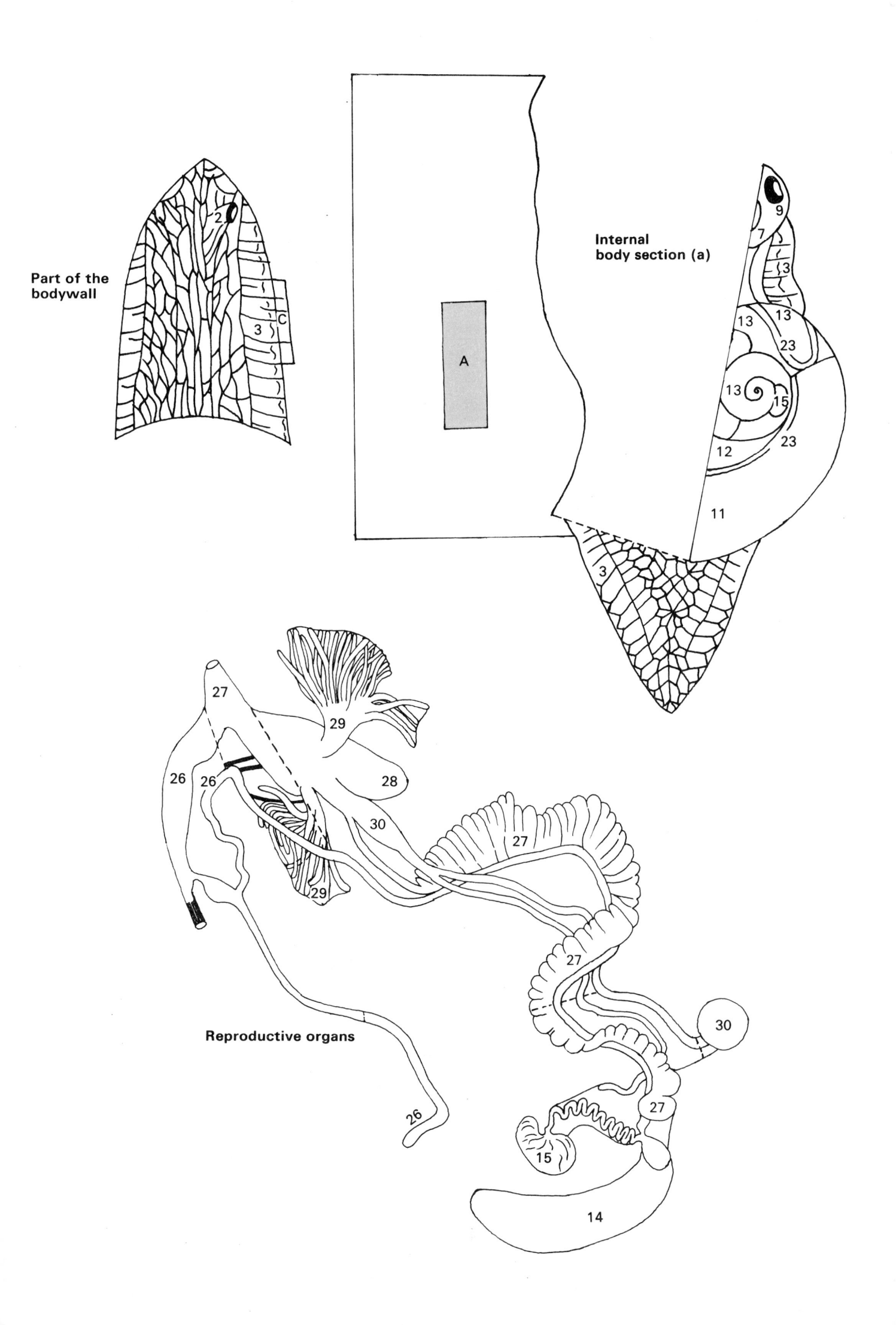

Part of the bodywall

Internal body section (a)

A

Reproductive organs